Magnificent Love:)

Personal Struggles

_____#LoveOn_____

—J. Michael Dekle

Copyright © 2016 Jonathan Dekle

www.jonathandekle.com Via Contact Us

ISBN: 0692776176
ISBN-13: 978-0692776179

DEDICATION

Here's to those who have struggled in life.
Who have questioned life.
This is my reflection of life.
I hope it can inspire you to know you are not
alone, and that love conquers all.
May these ideas, suggestions and conclusions
help guide you on as you walk through life's
struggles and challenges.

Table Of Content

Magnificent Love: Personal Struggles

Magnificent Love: Personal Struggles

Jonathan Dekle

ACKNOWLEDGMENTS

Thank you for choosing to read another of my books. I hope and pray you will be blessed by these words. Life's an adventure and we are always growing and becoming someone better. We all have been and still go through life's struggles. It is nice to know we are not the only ones. That many of us face such troubles all the time. For more positive empowering words: Follow one of my blogs Via

Instagram —
@jonnyslifeview

@sirnightwrites

@j.loveforeveru

@swiftnewsblog
&
@godscall1

Thank You
#PositiveVibes
#HeartVibes
#LoveOn

Why I Do What I Do

I don't do what I do for anything else besides I
love doing it.
Love helping others,
For by helping others I'm actually helping the
world plus myself.
Once you understand that—
Understand pure passion and love goes into
what I do and nothing less.
For I wouldn't do something and stand behind
it unless love goes forth with it.
—*J. Michael Dekle*

Ladder

Many days I awake and can fall into this hole.
The only way to get out of this hole is to climb
up the ladder.
This ladder being the ladder of positivity.
—*J. Michael Dekle*

I'll Be Me

I'll forever be me,
Be also the 'ME's' I hide—
Protected,
Rejected and neglected.
Me that saw and wish he could be.
I'll be all that I can be.
And within doing,
I hope I imagine off the happiest, most
funniest open honest loving caring person
people have yet to meet.
For if I can make you smile,
It'll make me smile.
If I can make you love,
It won't just make me love,
But love again and again over and over sharing
just how beautiful we all can be.
—*J. Michael Dekle*

Life Choices

Life's all about choices.
Remember what matters,
And what just passes and fades away.
For the things that last you can never buy;
For character and personality is irreplaceable,
Thus people is where it all matters.
—*J. Michael Dekle*

Quality of Life

Life's not about the amount of friends you
have in your life.
Nor the amount of money you have
or amount of anything really.
It's all about the quality and love within those
that truly matter.
I have encountered circles of people I have
associated with,
Work wise, friends, stranger, etc.
And what drew me in was the love.
Nothing else,
The love and passion they held and had.
The amount of money they made never
mattered—
Nor the amount of positivity they said didn't
even matter.
Not even the wild crazily done and said things
did either.
It was the love shown that mattered.
So to all those personally that have shown that
to me in my life,
Thank you.
Thank you for the love shown.
For someone like me,
It meant a million things.
It meant the world to me.

Emotions

It's when we let emotions fully control us
completely—
That we can completely loose ourselves.
Hoping we can find some parts of us in what
we just went into,
Because it's apart of us rather we like it or not.
We have a good side and a bad one.
Changing us depending on how each is being
used in the moment.
It's in these moments when everything matters
the most.
For so much of us is on the line, being shined
and shown to those he see.
Our actions speak volumes in the long run.
—*J. Michael Dekle*

Tip Toe

Tip toe through life.
Look and admire.
Let life do what it must.
Push what you must,
But choose those battles carefully.
For whatever you touch becomes a part of you
Affecting you one way or the other for ever.
For each lesson in life teaches.
Tip toe, so you know where you go.
Go as slow as you need,
But still staying going onward home—
Heavenwards.
—*J. Michael Dekle*

Repeated Time

Repeated time has a way of taking something
and making it stand in a different reality.
In a different perspective.
For you understand the feelings,
Know the outcome.
So for you to relive it as the first time becomes
harder and harder for you get to know it more
and more by doing it over and over.
That it becomes just normal.
Sometimes overly repetitive.
—J. Michael Dekle

Skies the Limit

Never limit what you think you can do,
For you can accomplish anything you seek.
Reach high,
Dream huge,
Fly on seeking upward wisdom.
God gives wisdom freely to those who ask.
Ask and believe, and it shall be yours.
—*J. Michael Dekle*

Stay You

Find that meaning to life:
And never let go of it.
Find who you are
Always reach to the heavens to find more of
who you are
For you never can stop growing and maturing,
It's an impossible thing!
Love life.
Love those who are apart of it!
Stay you.
Giving off love to all.
—*J. Michael Dekle*

Passion

Find your passions and turn that into
something that will help others,
But also help you,
For your doing what you love.
The more you see and live in life,
The more you know,
The more you can relate—
Creating a life takes time,
Creating a business takes time,
Building anything takes time.
And a lot of thought.
But you can do it,
If there's a will,
There's always a way.
Find a way,
Seek a way,
But stay trying,
And the way will be grooved into action.
Look above,
Look to love,
Look to God.
Let Him guide on.
—*J. Michael Dekle*

Doing

I have learned doing something spontaneous is
usually the best way to liven your life up and
keep you staying young
Or
If you just want to do something,
Just do it,
And see where it leads instead of second
guessing it.
Just jump and do.
Of course be reasonable and logical.
But don't let your fears hold you back.
Let your fears guide you on,
Telling you perhaps I can grow even more.
Let fear slowly make you become fearless.
—*J. Michael Dekle*

I'm The Type

I'm the type who'll love even when none is
given back.
The type who sees the bad,
But chooses the good.
The type who doesn't give up on someone
rather fights on for them.
I'm the type who loves so much,
That I become love crazy.
The type that tries' too stay as real as possible.
For my words and actions are all I got.
Is all that people can hold me to.
Yes sometimes,
I must back out,
Rethink,
Reroute, Redo.
But as long as the core me doesn't change.
I'll still stay me.
Loving;
Love—
Being,
Lil
Old
Me.
—*J. Michael Dekle*

Love Within

I have love within me that's so empowering
that my thoughts yet have found a way to
express it all—
Only that the feeling is so real.
That I can't help but live it,
And in time become more of love.
For the more you do something the more it
grows into you.
So the more you love, the more love will grow
on in you.
Love.
Live.
#LoveOn
—J. Michael Dekle

Big Heart

With such a big heart,
I fall in love with things so incredibly fast,
That when I see and touch something different
or amazing,
Or find something very fascinating;
I can't help but fall in love.
For it's helping me to explore more life,
And connect more realities.
Thus helping me grow in life.
Helping me to see how huge God is,
And how beautiful life truly really is.
—*J. Michael Dekle*

Deep Thoughts

When you have two deep thinkers,
That are passionate, caring, and hesitate; you
have two stubborn people aside each other.
You can have a lot of arguments that can
develop,
Because two heads can rub together and cause
tensions.
It's always good to have an understanding.
An even balance of discussion so there's a fair
good amount of time for each side to say their
side,
So jumping to conclusions can't happen.

—*J. Michael Dekle*

Be Yourself

When you truly allow yourself to be you,
Oh the beauty in it is priceless.
It's liberating.
When you have so much to share,
You could forever speak,
That's truly living.
Why worry what others will say about you,
Live by love.
Live by the Golden Rule;
And you will be loved,
Will be incredible being you.
Love God; Love all,
And all of life will be love.
For love will carry you through even the
hardest things in life.
That's something beautiful.
That's being genuine,
Being gorgeous.
Being you.
Something nobody should hide,
Are: (: Smiles :)
Some passion wanting to live.
The love we have inside us.
And never being afraid of sharing.
For sharing is caring :)

Beautiful Mind

Your mind is completely beautiful,
Never forget it.
I always wondered how you train your mind?
The way to do so,
Is simply by meditating on an idea for a while

—

If you're trying to forget,
All one must do is not dwell on the subject
anymore.
Instead find ways to think of other things.
I find that creating new hobbies,
Reading new books,
Etc.
Automatically starts to let your mind begin a
new page within itself.
Just by you allow it to move on to another
page.
Leaving the past thought stored away,
But away from you just simply allowing it to go
away by putting your focus onto something
that will help you in the present time.
Change, development, and progress all takes
time.
Leaving, if there's something you can't answer,
Simply allow yourself to admit it and walk on,
Knowing maybe one day you will be able to

understand it.
That you will find it's clarity in time.
For though you may forget for a while,
If ever you do find it;
It'll dawn on you like Christmas day.
I find writing thoughts of such lets my spirits
or emotions find a little clarity just in that until
that day of enlightenment comes.
It all adds to it self,
You add to yourself all the time,
By you reaching out and living life.
—*J. Michael Dekle*

Waiting

The hardest thing to do in life is to wait.
The best thing to do is uphold patients.
To stay busy so your mind doesn't think as
much.
For then you have peace within also.
Channel that mindset into another thought.
And then onto another and another until your
so mentally tired,
You can't even think.
It's called exercising your brain.
After all it is a muscle.

—*J. Michael Dekle*

Expressions

Sometimes I have trouble expressing myself.
When those moments occur,
I purely love it,
For it gives me a good puzzle to figure out,
Even if it drives me silly until I understand it.
I try my best to.
For if I can express myself better,
I can help others understand just that much
easier.
—*J. Michael Dekle*

Waiting Longer

Sometimes waiting is the only choice you have.
During the waiting time.
Leave the door open, but don't stop loving life,
Don't stop living and becoming the person you
always were going to become.
At the end of the day, all I ever want to do is
share my life with everyone and have you share
yours with me.
Leaving with both of us together, we would be
unstoppable.
Until then I'll fight for the both of us leaving
room for you always.
For what I want to do in life;
Is renew it with a whole new different view.
That leaves you asking:
Why haven't we seen it this way before?
—*J. Michael Dekle*

Sharing Life

All I want to do in life is live in the middle of
nowhere.
Being able to travel whenever and wherever.
Capturing life's moments.
Helping others gain a better understanding to
life in the process.
Having the love of my life next to me.
Laughing, loving, exploring, creating, visioning,
adoring, admiring, inspiring, empathizing, and
realizing how precious life is.
That it's meaningless if you have to only share
it with yourself.
That it's the people in your life that make it
truly incredible.
For me,
I only see one person I want to share it with
daily,
But will share with others also from afar.
Life is what you make it.
You must fight for what you want.
For evil will always try to tell you otherwise.
Life doesn't come to you,
You fight to live in it.
—*J. Michael Dekle*

Time is Time

Time is just time.
It's nearly impossible to change it.
For years to me are only seconds in my mind
sometimes.
Yes, waiting can hurt,
Can some days feel like forever,
But at the end of the day my heart and mind
know time has no hold over anything beside
this life.
For my heart lives in heaven.
Not here.
In the end,
It only expands my patients,
My love for God,
My understanding.
Allows me to accomplish other things in the
meantime.
So sometimes I wait,
And wait some more,
But know,
Whatever the wait is,
It is worth it.
And the time in-between the wait;
Isn't wasted but used carefully.
—*J. Michael Dekle*

One Day

One day soon I'll travel everywhere.
I'll travel and write about it all.
Discovering new places incredible.
Not worrying about a single thing;
Besides where to go next.
Thinking on how can I show more of Gods
love?
How can I better serve others?
After traveling for a while,
I'll settle down out in the middle of nowhere.
I don't need anyone to make me happy.
I have heavens happiness in my heart.
Doesn't mean I wouldn't enjoy the company.
I won't ask for anyone to be next to me.
For it's their choice to be or not.
I'm planning my life now:
I always am;
For there's always something more to
accomplish.
But life is made to be shared.
For others bring life to actual life.
Surround yourself with joy from others.
—*J. Michael Dekle*

Travel On

As I travel,
I love passing 'ghost towns'
Towns that used to be full of excitement.
For it tells me possessions and empires, etc.
They all pass away,
Fading away leaving trash and ashes.
It's why valuing the people in your life is so
important.
It's why investing in love ones is where the
true meaning of life happens.
Why investing in heaven by accepting Jesus is
so incredible.
Be successful—
But until you have a family,
You truly haven't gained any success at all.
Seek love,
Seek friendships,
Seek God.
For that's where you will find happiness.
—*J. Michael Dekle*

New Lessons

Each day I learn something new.
Life slowly is becoming easier and easier.
It's as though the books have shifted from
difficult to easy,
And now I read, "Hello."
Meaning I must dig deeper,
So life will still stay a challenge,
So it's as though I'm reading a foreign book.
Challenge accepted!
Adding on to myself.
Learning new wonders to life.
Connecting each reality even more.
—*J. Michael Dekle*

All Your Choices

Once you see it's all you,
And only you,
You understand adulthood.
For connections help us,
But sometimes limit us from growing
ourselves.
Others will help,
Can contribute to our growth.
But never rely on them,
Rather appreciate and enjoy them while they
are nearby.
Only rely on God.
Humans can disappoint.
We are not perfect.
Choose those carefully to fully trust.
And love all, always.
—*J. Michael Dekle*

Underestimates

When someone underestimates you,
It tells you more about them than imaginable,
For if they are already underestimating you,
Just imagine how they do it to themselves with
such negativity ruling their point of view.
Send hope.
Send inspiration.
We already have too much negativity.
We need more positivity in life.
So our eyes can be more opened,
To see others points of uplifting ideas—
To see all the love and hope in the world;
Filled with ways to solve the unprecedented
realities pressing in on us.
Take others inspiration and ideas.
Basing them off the Golden Rule;
And love for humanity is what you will get.
Let's not underestimate each other rather be
honest and help each other up to places truly
incredible.
Speak our past done lessons,
Leave the past in the past,
But be open enough about it so you can
express the lessons learned so others can be
forewarned about its pros and cons.
Each soul is a lesson book.

Let your soul speak its words of advice.
Be willing to listen to others.
For Sharing is Truly Caring.
Let's be expressive with loving gestures rather
than hating de-lowering words.
Let's love on!
—*J. Michael Dekle*

Ask yourself this:
Have you underestimated yourself?
Have you had such disbelief in yourself that
you think you're not capable of anything truly
great in life?
Don't let someones words define you.
Rather take their words and let them help give
you better perspectives on how you may
actually be currently acting.
Never take some strangers words to heart,
For they only see the surface,
Never seeing the whole of you fully.
The struggling moments bringing you through
to get you to now are needed for your growth.
We are human, we mess up more often then
we would like to admit, but we still do it.
Council in someone close to you, who knows
you deeply.
Honesty has power many do not like,
But accept it and spend the time needed to

reflect it so you can make sense of yourself
better, so you will be also more understood.
As you accept your past, your current self, it
lets you move on forward with clarity.
Seek God daily; pray daily; He listens always.
He knows you better than you know yourself.

Want to truly have a sound life?
Seek God daily.
Now in return:
Give everyone respect for their life song
journey.
Do not judge, for 10 out of 10 you never will
know their full life story.
You do not know what they had to face daily,
Who was their roll model shaping them into
who they are today.
What surrounding influences they had to dwell
in day in to day out.
We all are broken in one way or another.
And nothing is wrong with that.
We live in a sinful world, were good and evil
truly lives on.
Seek after being the good, shunning away the
evil and peace in mind and heart will be your
end result.
#LoveOn.
—*J. Michael Dekle*

Key Treasure

You can give someone a free key to something
incredible,
But you can't make them open that door,
No matter how amazing the treasure is inside,
They have to choose to take that leap of faith
to gain such even if it is offered to them freely.
Jesus offers a treasure beyond our
imaginations, Heaven.
It's free, we just have to choose to accept His
love and grace for us.
His forgives and loves us always,
We just must love Him for Him too.
—*J. Michael Dekle*

Lonely One

To sit as a strange one.
To see the world through different eyes.
The loneliness that comes can almost
suffocate.
The misunderstanding towards the hateful
poor tortured souls is endless.
By being so separated from everyone else,
but so connected to everything else,
You feel every emotional level imaginable.
You can understand the unthinkable.
The untouchable.
For you can touch each soul.
For the strange that you are,
Is your old soul,
Being in such a fallen world.
Stay you, genuine.
Stay loving;
Be forgiving.
Love on always.
—*J. Michael Dekle*

Ђeart Crushed

He walked head down.
Sadden deeply.
His heart so heavy words are hard to say aloud.
He felt as though his heart has been crushed.
As soon as it was crushed it rushes to repair.
Repairing itself so fast,
That nobody can ever truly break him.
Sadden someone would play such a game as
that.
He knows deep down,
They wouldn't if they only knew the love sent
was realer than real.
Was heaven sent.
So real you feel it in the air.
Instead of letting it break him,
He let himself feel more pity than ever before
for the human race.
Yes, his mind races and chases his enemies,
But says he only wants to be friends with all.
He looks out and with his head down says it's
okay, I forgive the haters.
He will love them all anyway.
Every atom in him tells him to crush and
destroy them.
For that's all he felt from them.
Love calls him and calms him.

Tells him it will be okay.
That their payday will come, and when it does,
They will pray for mercy.
And there will be none to give,
For they never gave any.
He begging maybe they would change their
ways before it's to late.
So he prays each day for them.
Hoping it may save them.
For even if heartache somedays may be his
drink of daily walk,
He still prays love and grace will be theirs.
—*J. Michael Dekle*

Anytime someone hurts you, puts you down,
or leaves you with heartbrokenness—
remember these words. Everyone is journeying
on. Each persons steps in life is different. It is
not our place to judge nor to try to give
payback, it's only God's. Be the love; be the
grace, the one who forgives, who then forgets.
Do it for yourself, for if you try to give
everyone their 'payback' you will never be fully
happy in life, for there will always be those
who will mistreat you.
Learn which battles to fight, and which to just
let go of.
#LoveOn.

An Authors Life

Being able to write and express feelings and
life in so many different ways can be strange.
It leaves someone to view you in a certain way.
Leaving them forgetting that a true writer lives
in many ways.
For they make it their job to step into different
shoes.
When they write, they truly capture its beauty.
They take the shoes off and step back into
their own when they can.
Many never get to see their own shoes they
wear on a daily.
But those lucky few who do,
Are always blown away,
For they have such a wide view on life,
Have such a connection to people,
That they seem almost inhuman.
For they are so widely spread-out as a being,
For how they are made,
How their minds work,
They have this glow of wonder to them.
For they feel everything.
They love so supremely,
That they can't help but release its beauty.
But since they are so different,

They live a lot of the time alone.
When in reality they would love to have others
as company.
But they have such a drive in them,
That if alone they must be,
They can,
For they were made to lead.
Made to guide.
But imagine a few different beings coming
together.
Imagine what could be accomplished.
I love all people.
Intelligence and true genuine kindness is the
most attractive vibe.
But also the passion that is behind their
actions is beautiful to the soul.
Anyone can be a genius in something;
Be a genius in whatever you're passionate
towards.
When I look into others eyes,
I see all that I am not,
And love everything about it.
For it tells me,
I'm still only learning and growing.
Grow off others passions.
For any passion has life to it.
—J. Michael Dekle

Reality

It's a sad reality:
The more you reach out,
The more you regret,
For you begin to wonder was it worth reaching
out?
Did I do the best I could have done?
Was it me,
Or just them?
Could we of done something better?
Would we of become better?
I leave all these questions for you—
Believe in what you're trying to do,
And put aside others approval—
For they will never approve when they can't
see what you see.
As long as your vision is planned,
Organized and fully pushed till completion,
You truly can accomplish anything.
For once God fully guides your life,
Your life flies spiritually.
Flies physically;
Mentally —just in all ways.
That's Gods power.
—*J. Michael Dekle*

I Could

I could stop now,
And the fight would go.
I could stop, but if I would stop,
You never would have a clue to what that
would fully mean.
Everyone is made to do something.
Never expect anything from anyone.
For people will crush you over and over with
their lack of compassion.
Their lack of kindness and love.
Never think of someone as perfect.
While look at yourself and see if it's
acceptable before saying anything,
Then look at God,
Then speak.
—*J. Michael Dekle*

Dark Valleys

Though I walk through the valley of death,
I'll forever love.
Though I talk with monsters,
I'll forever forgive.

Though life will show many colors,

My banner will show peace.

Though I don't know my next exit and entry,
I'll forever walk doing all I can do bettering all

and anything I touch.

For love lives on—

Lives on in song,
In our palms by us letting our love flow out

flowering its power.

Looking up praying dear God.

Am just me.

Yet it leaves me wanting to express such words
the world will never be the same once I'm

done.

For my passion will capture life,

Trapping them forever in words,
Leaving my actions to be expressed

automatically.

Leaving me to ask,

Who's riding with?
—*J. Michael Dekle*

Ђappy Cry

I rarely cry—
I feel like it everyday usually—
But to cry over just how beautiful something
can go together,
For you know God directed such.
The feeling isn't explainable.
Just so real.
—*J. Michael Dekle*

Lights Ray

Once you see where you fit in the whole
picture of life,
And understand its role,
You begin to find purpose and fulfillment in
the process.
You see the pros and the cons,
But always deep down wonder why God made
you the way He did?
In the sense we all are special,
But within each special soul is something only
they carry,
The question is:
Does that sparkle of spark light itself off?
Or is it still hidden and finding itself,
So it can in confidence.
—*J. Michael Dekle*

Life's Compass

It's absolutely incredible how life works out.
Leaving you knowing God is in control.
I have noticed,
It's in those moments where things seem to be
falling completely apart,
Is when they start to make sense,
And the flight to a better place happens.
For you allow it to take place.
Within yourself,
By seeking God to live in there also.

—*J. Michael Dekle*

No Negativity

I refuse to allow any atom of disbelief to stay
in me!
I refuse to take any negativity in my being and
believe it!
I refuse to wait another day to take a stand,
To make a change,
To enact an idea.
For today is the day to do what you must do,
For tomorrow is not promised.
Today say, do, and make it count to its fullest
maximum as though it was your last day.
For then you know you gave your all,
All the time.
Leaving no regrets.
Find clarity in each action before heading
fourth.
Love,
Have passion and understanding go forth with
you.
It will guide you,
God will.
—*J. Michael Dekle*

Gods Love

Even if dark days come.
I will not let go of the love from above.
I will forever give all my heart to God even if
some days the blindness on doing so is
unknown.
I know my faith is weak,
But my courage to walk on,
To move on,
To show better love to all,
It drives me,
Ties me to the will to want to do so.
My flesh is weak,
But my seeking to perfection is so high that
even if I fall a billion times,
The will to keep moving forever on leads me
on.
That the life I have been given has so much
potential,
So much insightful wisdom bestowed.
Leaving to ask: —
How could I be so blessed?
How could I be so strong?
How could I be so stubborn that it makes me
stupid some days?
How could I be so different?
Yet so ever connected that I can touch

anyone's heart.
Is it that it is my gift to everyone,
To share such passion with such convention
that it moves anyone—
Moves mountains?
Some days I wonder how much is me, and how
much is You.
For even if my mind and my actions can
detour off course,
You know my heart and read my heart.
The patients You have is beyond
understanding.
The love You give is so freely,
So irreplaceable,
So connected.
You all are so special, so irreplaceable to God,
That know you are beyond loved.
He has a place for you, forever, with forever
serving services of work that doesn't seem like
work,
For it's so much fun,
There's so much contentment and purpose in
heaven, even in this life.
It's what life all about.
Even if now sorrow and pain hurts you,
Follows you,
Know how we live in such a sinful world that
it's God way of preparing you for what's to

come.
The time of troubles,
They will come, but they won't last.
Remember that.
They will only fade away.
Life's filled with confusion,
With sickness, greed, pride, selfishness and
disaster.
But with Gods upmost love,
Even in those moments the amount of
blessings is forever empowering to the soul.
Are a forever reminder of love.
God knows all,
Just trust His ways.
And watch the blessings He gives so freely.
—*J. Michael Dekle*

Perhaps

Maybe it would seem things haven't worked
yet?
That life has given you more lemons than
melons?
Perhaps you haven't fully followed what you
know is right?
Maybe you had to learn some lessons the hard
way?
Perhaps have feared of something.
Anything is possible.
Life comes at you in all sort of ways.
Trust Him.
Trust love.
Trust Heavens way.
I wish I fully could say more.
All I know is, each challenge in life only makes
us stronger.
Not weaker.
Keep the faith.
#LoveOn
—*J. Michael Dekle*

Responsibility

When you have so much on the plate,
It leaves you like,
"Oh man, where to even begin!"
That's when you know you think too much,
and have too many dreams.
It's like filling your plate so full,
You stare at it for five minutes and figure out
what you're going to eat first,
Then second, etc…
Then you begin to eat that food!
Eat that next project,
By applying yourself and doing it.
Being responsible with the talents you have
been given.
Let them drive you on.
So life is fulfilling.
—*J. Michael Dekle*

Life Will Test

Life will test you.
Things will come that you can never control,
They just happen.
During each trail, each coming challenge, we
have choices to make.
We get to choose how we will handle them.
How our emotions will determine our
releasing actions.
Life will test you every single day.
Learn God controls it all,
Leaving everything happens for a reason.
Just breathe, examine, understand, and then
move on forward with whatever is happening.
If you just enact off impulse, more likely than
not, you will regret something later down the
road.
Someone may be hurt by your words, bridges
may be burnt, misunderstandings may happen.
Life will test, past each one by staying calm.
Knowing sunshine suns on after every storm.
#LoveOn
—*J. Michael Dekle*

Day by Day

Day by day I close my eyes and pray to God
for some higher power GPS guidance.
Way by way I sometimes glide off to get
distracted by life falling away to the dances.
Awaking having to take second glances and
saying…
Wait wait—
What!
Why did I just do that and that and end up on
that hell pathway once again?
Friends pointing fingers on me putting me on
some high-end quality quoted pole expecting
me to understand everything in reality format.
All I can say is I try and try to fight and fight
on and on to keep my senses together so I can
at least try to better things.
If I fall here and there;
It's not who I am,
It's simply my staidness coming out trying to
show my other side that try's to hide and ride
me on to some death pride ride.
Trying to pull me back into the middle,
So fighting on in this tug a war becoming the
warrior.
Life's about living truly free or dying trying.
It's about choosing sides.

Which side do you choose?
Good or Evil?
God or the devil.
I choose God, for He is good,
He loves unconditionally.
Loves you no matter what.
You just get to choose who you serve.
Your daily actions show all who you serve.
Some days we choose wrongly,
But nothing is wrong with that if you then
choose to learn the lessons from such and
move on now stronger and better.
Love On, and if you love on, God is with you,
For God is love.
—*J. Michael Dekle*

#LoveOnForever
#JesusIsLove
#YouAreLovable
#PositiveVibes
#PositiveLife
#YouGotThis
#KeepGoingOn
#LoveOn

Mind Battle

Life will always challenge you to push each
limitation you have to make it seem
impossible.
So many people underestimate their brain
power,
If you would just exercise it.
You could use it so much more creatively,
logically, spiritually, and mentally.
Did you know it's a scientific fact that if you
read just to read;
Reading more informational life-related
situations is my suggestion, but any type of
reading—
You will naturally become more creative,
And more able to connect things,
Have more of an ability to just live life and feel
a little smarter.
The reason is,
People are wired just like electrical wire is
wired in some senses, let me example.
You have to channel and imprint different
ways to the brain so you can fully understand,
But moreover,
Simply remember;
Electrical wire doesn't choose where it goes, it
has to be placed carefully where it belongs,

following codes and regulations so it all works
probably and safely.
If you read, and see and hear all at the same
time,
Your likelihood of learning anything is double,
tripled.
What you choose to read and watch, etc. is the
data in the electrical wire for what your mind
will transmit its data out by your actions and
words, the more you learn, the larger those
wire connections get. Same with electric wire,
the more power going through, the bigger the
wire needs to be to hold it all it's power.
How you think and discipline your mind in
doing so, is you carefully placing down the
hard wire for your minds system of function.
The codes and regulations is common sense
guiding you in how to do so safely.
Gods wisdom and the Golden Rule is a good
guide to live by at all times.
Now if the wires are connected correctly you
will have true power.
So in return it all connects. If you train your
mind correctly, and filled it with inspiration,
love, kindness, and God, etc,
Your mind and life will work peacefully
without worry.
Organization is key.

So why watch useless information?
Why read the useless information?
When you could learn by simply living life.
By watching and reading content you find to
love anyways.
Simply create hobbies you like,
Find your inner passions.
Subjects you wish to gather more information
on, and research after.
Google that amazing content!
Once you slowly learn new things—
You will have more capabilities you can do in
life because your perspective is just that much
larger, that much more together & connected.
Go out and seek wisdom, seek knowledge,
become enlightened today!
Become more enriched in your life!
Adventure and reading empowering content as
often as you can will only help you in life!
Get Her Done Today!
Get Life Started!
Get Fulfillment!
Then of course, keep living it,
And doing it!
Perhaps you want to master certain fields,
Apply yourself on a more academic level and
learn and grow and moreover help empower
others to do so also.

The mind is free,
Want to solve problems,
Start using your head,
Sounds funny I know,
But really think about it,
It makes since.
Once you do,
You will realize freedom.
Many find this freedom,
By not being afraid to try new things,
And more or less not being afraid to reach
failure so they can eventually make success.
So they try on and battle on until they
understand they can either do it,
Or learn lessons from it.
What you read,
Watch, listen,
And pay your attentional focus to,
You will slowly become.
Maybe not right away,
So if you pay attention to none sense all the
time—
It's as though you have stopped and you're
digging a hole.
It's as though life hit a repeat and you began to
walk a circle.
How many ways do I need to say it?
If you follow a path that is already created, you

will walk a circle my friends.
Young ones—
Grow in understanding,
Grow in God,
In love,
In freedom of choice,
Follow kindness, morals,
And the Ten Commandments,
And you will find happiness,
Forever peace,
For you will be at peace.
So crazy how simple,
Yet how hard we make it.
Now let me add,
And really add.
I'm not saying not to watch anything,
To not play games,
To not do completely nonsense craziness,
I'm just saying balance.
A balanced life is a happy one,
This saying didn't just fall from the sky,
It really has a valued point.
Key points:
Exercise your brain as you would any muscle,
But fill it with knowledge and you,
As in learn you,
Understand who you are.
Take a 16 personality test,

Let the test guide you, but do not let it define
you!
And read and do you,
Add morals into it all,
In whatever you do,
Do it as though it is for yourself,
To reach a higher level,
As though it was for your Mother,
Your wife, your husband, etc.
Reach more, now higher,
As if it was for God,
Who created you,
And gave you a place in His Kingdom if you
choose Him.
Some make it sound like God isn't fair,
Let me ask then:
How many live and act God?
Live in His reflection perfectly?
No one does.
So stop looking at any type of human as
though they are God, for they are not, and will
disappoint every single time.
We all mess up and thus can learn from our
mess ups and become better.
How many don't even follow God now?
So imagine how God could look so dead with
a people who don't follow or believe Him.
God lets you live your choices,

Lets you live the way you want to,
But He will let you reap what you sow.
If you sow self,
You will be selfish.
If you sow greed,
You will be greedy.
If evil, evil.
If good things, then goodness.
If kind things, then kindness.
If love, then love.
And so on—
You reap whatever you sow;
Whatever you act and do.
So be you, and be as you would treat yourself.
Put God into place first for He made you,
For you are special and have reason to be alive
in this world,
And His to come, Heaven.
Many forget this,
So it's easy to say Self is more alive and well.
God does not say to not be self,
We just tend to forget self and God go hand in
hand.
It's a marriage, you become one.
So you more or less create a happy and
peaceful life wherever you go in God.
Remember God,
For He is the only one who created such

sensible laws and realization to life and the
cycling ways we are made to live.
Which is forever,
Why live a forever repeat?
We are made to be all,
Made in Gods imagine.
Made to reflect and worship God,
To be able to grow and understand God more,
Thus slowly ourselves be His imagine of
reflection to all we come across.
Leaving you really capable of really anything
imaginable under the Son,
If you simply give God the respect you would
a God, you will start to see God better.
God will give you anything under the sun if
you worship Him as the one who gave the sun,
moon and stars and all of life and all things in
life, actually living power and life.
He will trust you with all things.
Thus help you achieve all things.
Believe Him, trust Him, and life is yours.
Now whatever you turn into a "god" is
whatever you pay the most attention too....
Now think how sad God is when He looks
and sees when nobody focuses on Him purely.
Yes this life doesn't allow us to all the time
focus on God, but we still get to choose if we
will bring Him into our focal view.

If we will spend the time with Him in His
Bible, in prayer.
Some could say, why is there such people who
clearly aren't of God so highly great?
It's that their "god" is the devil.
And yes the devil is a god,
For God gave him powers of a god,
But of earth, king, and master,
But for a very short time.
The same structure as in Heaven.
But corrupted completely.
Look out into society, you will see evil, see it
very clearly once you begin to look.
It's out of pure love God still allows such
evilness to even be around.
If you really think about it.
Evilness equals,
Hurt, pain, sadness, meanness, anger,
depression, anxiety, anything negative.
If you really think deep down,
Those don't help you in life.
Some of us live in such mental and physical
places that to survive we actually learn to love
those feelings of negative for it's all we know,
All we understand,
We trust the feeling,
We humans run off feelings,
For it's the only way we feel alive,

We live off it, and some of us never try to
leave it, we live off it some more,
Off it's energy.
Some throw people's emotions away like trash,
Saying, no, you can't do that!
No, you're not pretty, you're not smart, you're
not anything, you're just regular, you are just a
normal person, maybe you are the worst there
ever was, your mean, you're horrible, why
would you do that, how could you, I hate you,
I will end you, I never want to see you again, I
don't love you, how stupid, how immature!
You see how negative that all is?
Instead of saying,
Hey, you could do this, this way—
Well, I don't like that because—
Give reason to what you say,
So understanding is made.
Many fight themselves.
I'm stupid,
No you're not!
Just keep trying, you will get there—
If you see why negativity could kill anyone you
will understand why things are the way they are
in the world with good and evil living.
Understanding the battle between good and
evil which really means;
Once you understand this in itself,

You fully see why the Devil would hate us so
very much,
For we are soon to be angels,
Which is what he used to be, an angel of God,
But he lost it all, becoming an angel of evil.
Gave it all away for his own little "heaven."
Once Eve and Adam took of the forbidden
fruit, the devil gain control of earth, as king,
master and ruler.
When Jesus came and died for us, that was
broken, the key to freedom was fully given to
all, if they choose God full heartily.
But the devil still has his reign till Jesus comes
to take us home, thus why good and evil still
live on till this very day.
Let me ask:
If you were the devil and had such power
wouldn't you try to teach your ways to all?
Serve people—
Influences them,
But since you don't carry Gods love in your
heart, but darkness…
You do more negative,
Think on more of a selfish want—
That's the devil for you.
All he ever wanted was to be treated as a god,
and do what a god does, which is to rule.
If you were a ruler, wouldn't you have your

own laws, own everything in your own image?
After all it would be your reflection and
interpretation of how life should be—-
Now look out again at the world, and see what
his kingdoms brings?
Anything bad you can blame the devil, the
father of sin and lies.
Hunger, pain, suffering, death, greed, pride etc.
belongs to the devil.
God is all but loving, all but pure and good.
Anything bad you see, understand God didn't
want to ever happen, but has allowed to
happen to prove to all, how wrong and
stupidly foolish it is to think you could ever be
God and know what to do, and when to do it,
etc.
Sin is as cancer, it's unknown at first, but once
it takes hold, it grows and spreads everywhere.
Now understand the parallels of worship here,
yet see how extremely different they truly are.
If you don't fully worship and follow satan, he
will not grant you everything in this world.
What do I mean?
The devil owns a lot, he owns anything
materialistic.
Can give you it if you choose him.
But see, he does not own your mind, your
freedom of thoughts and what truly matters,

your characteristics.
He can only pollute and deliver you his way of
life, via media and other ways.
Why do you think media is so huge?
He can suggest evil, and you can then thus
enact what you see out into your actions.
I'm not saying all media is bad, for the devil
usually puts 90% good with the 10% bad, so
you slowly are dumbed, numbed and see it all
as justifiable. His a snake, never forget.
But look years ago, what is acceptable now,
people years ago would never had accepted,
For they followed God more, followed rules
and codes that kept peace and honor among us
and shunned evil away.
God owns everything.
God gives wisdom more than He does
materialistic things, the reason is; many do not
know how to control themselves with
materialistic things, and it leads to downfalls,
leading to being more selfish, etc.
Wisdom helps you see the difference between
good and evil for what they truly are.
All that matters in this life is choosing God.
After that, it's all blessings given from God
that we usually take without thinking.
If you worship and follow God,
God will give you all those things, for He

created all those things.
Remembering God only gives us what we can
handle, which is beautiful once understanding.
Remember satan is "Earth's god".
He has made things too through us,
But only earthly things,
For this is his playing grounds he is allowed to
do his work on it.
Much said, sorry.
God usually doesn't bestow riches for He
knows we will forget Him. The saying money
is the root of all evil is true because most of
us can't handle money responsibly. Many hate
hearing this, but it's very true. God bestows
wisdom more than He does anything else.
Wisdom helps you understand realities and sin
easier. Once you respect God and fully can live
by what you know of Him, God will give you
everything you can imagine. Sadly, how many
of us fully give God our time, our devotion
and respect fully and daily Him?
Reread for its empowering to those who truly
want to understand and grow and become
peaceful, and understand the differences
between good and evil.
God equals forever happiness,
Bestowing rich-fullness in all ways of riches of
character & love.

That's something incredible.
Don't live in hell when you don't have to.
God's Heaven we can't even imagine yet.
—*J. Michael Dekle*

If You Fall

Sometimes what happens to the truest of
hearts and souls is we reach a breaking point.
We have two choices.
We either allow the crushing pressure to break
us or turn us into diamonds.
Many of us fall,
All turning into diamonds as we fall.
As we fall we realize in time that a heart as
ours goes from pure good to pure evil.
For if we don't learn to forgive, forget, we
slowly start to hate—
If we allow.
As we fall more to rock bottom.
We fall and lean into the dark side,
Into the negativity that it consumes our very
soul if we don't watch out.
If we agree with what we hear negatively, sadly
we do a lot of the time, it can be damaging.
A selected few fight the demons plus the
world, for many hate the truth, hate what they
do not understand, which is natural to feel.
Turning those who fight against all odds into

the highest levels of light the world will ever
see if they believe and follow God.
As the world judges and tries to bring them
back down to hells bottom,
They find their rock bottom is God,
God slowly helping to make them diamonds.
For they become truly unstoppable.
Instead of letting the bad consume them,
They fight to still show love and goodness.
But for them to achieve and get to such a
point of understanding and commitment,
They must reject every ones negative bad point
of view towards them that has ever been done
to their souls, closing the past away.
Shunning away the negativity of disbelief in
their own minds outward perspective.
For they have to be grounded solidly in what
they believe in and stand for it.
Then they can come back,
And stand with everyone,
Being truly unbreakable and unstoppable.
For them to do that,
They become the loneliness,
For by that point no human can interfere with
them for they have to battle self,
They must find themselves,
But find themselves with God as their Leader.
For they have leagues of demons of all levels

after them by then,
Influencing all and any they encounter.
If they allow,
They can call upon God and have many more
leagues of heavenly angels as their company—
But then,
To get to such a point,
You will test yourself over and over and over.
As in your disbelief, self doubt will test you.
If you believe God will help you, guide you,
He will fully, He always is, but if you call upon
Him, He will even more for you give Him
power in your life to do so.
God's always by your side, but if you want to
grow more and more with God, believe full
heartily in Him, but also in yourself.
God and you go hand in hand in that sense.
I wish faith was just a part of us, but the more
damaged we get, the harder we trust, thus
usually the less we have faith God is right next
to us in those difficult times.
If our faith is firm in God.
Firm in what we seek to do, we will be able to
do it easier, for God is by us helping.
God will make a way when He sees fit..
Staying positive is key no matter the storm.
God will always be right next to you,
Rather you feel Him or not.

He is always by you,
Once you know this,
Your faith itself just jumped higher than
before, for you gave Him more control in your
life to help you, dropping pride and self is key.
To those who still doubt this though,
Many fall back,
And when they fall back,
Their disbelief can hurt them deeply.
Sometimes many end up joining the demons
way of thinking and living without even fully
realizing they are, for they begin to rely on self.
For they feel like no one is for them.
If you listen to the negative more than you do
the positive, it's as though you are listening to
the devil more than God.
It's wild once you understand this.
Truly enlightening to know.
God won't even reveal Himself directly
sometimes during our disbelief moments.
For He can't,
For if He would,
It wouldn't be true genuine faith and belief.
It would be a false one.
A forced one.
God doesn't force anything.
He will only guide on through the Bible.
Some may not understand this,

Read the story of Job,
You will see more to what I say.
But those who do,
Will you forever fight on?
For if you fall,
Believe me,
You won't ever come back the same,
For you will be long gone in all those ways.
You will be that broken to that reality.
You will have to be,
To understand why you fell and failed.
Leaving why God lets the 'struggles' become
so real at times in our lives,
So God Himself can become that much more
realer with you and that much more alive in
your personal journey and walk with Him.
Once you finally understand everything that
has happened in your life has a reason;
Seeing it all had its place,
Time and purpose,
And the overall power to help shape you into
the strongest person needed to be to face this
world of fallen sickness, you truly have
become enlighten with God's help and life will
slowly make more sense as time passes.
This sense of peace will come across you, for
you no longer fight self and God, you finally
walk next to God, and see Him as your

Mentor, Leader and Savior.
The more you fall and the more you call to
God, the more you will become enlightened.
God can give you insight to how you failed,
But on your side of it, you must take the time
to reflect upon it, and do so praying to God to
help give such insight back.
It's why this life will always have it's valleys and
hilly challenges, so you can truly understand
the battle between good and evil.
—*J. Michael Dekle*

You never know when you may see
someone, or hear from them. You never know
when you will be able to do and accomplish
something either. Time is precious, is valuable,
is made to be used preciously. Each second
wasted wrongly is done so freely by your
choices.

Life is a gift from God to even have, to
calm as your own. But He loves us so much—
that He allows us to choose freely everything
we do. Good or wrong. He will allow you to
choose what you do down to your very death.

Yes, if you allow Him, He will guide you,
show you in His time and in His wisdom the

understanding to all of life's problems. That He is always trying to protect you to the highest amount at all times in your daily life.

The problem and trouble many of us have are we tend to not trust as much as we could in God. For we naturally trust only ourselves to the highest degree, that full submission of self, it has to be dropped, thus humbled; it is the hardest thing a human will ever have to do, but once self is fully dropped, the enlightenment can start to happen. For that means you're teachable and willing to listen to God so fully that He can talk so directly to you, for He knows whatever He says, you will listen and hear, and fully follow, for you only want to obey Him, your Master, your Creator of all things, now, and that will forever be made!

God will protect you, just follow Him, He will bless you, just listen to Him. Follow His commands, for they are justice. Act His ways, for they are correct and honorable. They are designed to bring you a happy life, a meaningful purposefully powerful life.

For we are soon angels, are at heart angelic beings, kings and queens, that is if we follow

God and be His messengers, His teachers, mentors, leaders, and followers, we will surely have a place in heaven. Not a heaven on this earth, for heaven can only live in our hearts here on earth. That God and His legions of uncountable angels of light will be your guide through this life till Jesus comes in the clouds of heavens.

Yes, the ride will be hard, tough, rough and even deathly, but to die for God here on earth is never a waste. To die in belief, trust and the best you can be to God is to die knowing you will awake and see God face to face coming in the clouds of heavens telling you...... "Well done, well done, my precious child! Well done, well done, welcome, welcome home son, daughter!" What a day that will be—

If you live with that moment always captured in your mind, that love has set us free forever, for Jesus's love of dying on the cross paid for sin and all if we accept Jesus as our Lord and Savior, the peace you will have is beyond words to express besides beautiful.

We can call upon God for mercy, for forgiveness, for grace, for His overwhelming love, for understanding, knowledge and a better understanding to why we are still here on earth living in such a time as this daily. Just pray to God daily for spiritual enlightenment.

We are here still to share Gods love; to be His reflection; to be such mirrors — people see us and they see God, see heaven, for we have such love that we can't help but express it, share it, be it, that we shall sing it! Never hide God, never think God isn't awesome, for He is sooo—AWESOME!

Follow His ways, for He loves His children who obey His commandments, loves to award, protect, bless, help, comfort, and give wisdom to all, you just must seek after Him daily.

Be real with yourself, so God can be real to you. Pray to God dearly to help show you your own reflection, and take the cup of surfing that comes with. What do I mean the cup of surfing? Your own sinful reflection. For many, it won't be so bad, but for others, the reflection can almost kill! The cup is so old to bitter, so sorrowful, so incredibly heartbreaking, that it pains you so incredibly much, that you are just so incredibly thankful that God says, "But son, daughter, you are forgiving; let Me show you your new reflection in Me, let Me teach you, train you, help you know of My ways. For I Am Love, I Am the I Am. The only way to forever lasting life, to forever lasting peace. I love you, let Me into your heart to teach you, and help guide you. I Am knocking, will you hear Me?" —Jesus.

Pray to God every second of the day, as much as possible, as in say, God, I'm back, you there? And begin thinking again thoughts with God, and thus real true genuine prayer is being done. It's so awesome to know how easy it is to talk to God. It's why a quite place is so amazing. Why music with no words, no beat, but the pure sound is so soothing while thinking and meditating and reflecting deep personal life and spiritual related problems.

Music with beats, words, it scrambles your thoughts, you still think, etc, but it's not as clear, as in God isn't, yourself is for sure, even the Devils is, it's why his music is everywhere, when we hear God through even all that, it's God calling so loud, that no one can stop His voice, no one. When He wants to talk to you, He will no matter what, but as a flashing at first or a flashing of warning, concernment within our thoughts and emotions; if we bypass it, God leaves, for we choose to do us and enact on what we want rather taking heed to God, which leaves God sadden deeply.

It's why we must accept and be so openly talking to God, that He guides our thoughts almost fully, by that point, you are such of dearest friends. It's why it pains God so much when we walk away from Him when we do not spend enough time reading His Words. For it's praying while reading, for God can talk to you still, but even more so when you read His Bible. His Bible is living life if you invite Him into your daily reading. So read daily......

I challenge everyone this. Before reading your Bible next, stop and ask God what to read, and He will tell you in seconds. I find this to be the best way to study my Bible. At the end of the day, only you can answer to you. When you think about it in that way, you have to come across it as so incredibly precious, so meaningful, so honorable that you choose your life fully. For you choose it all down to your death. That how could you dare even want to waste it! I know myself, I have wasted such precious time that could have been so breathtakingly beautiful, just if I wouldn't have been so foolish and selfish, that it is beyond heart aching to admit once thinking about it.

Lucky with technology it's possible, but life and death are never a known thing. So just love everyone and always be the best friend as possible, for you never know when you may see each other again, so always smile and laugh, and help each other become the best as possible to one another. For it's what a friend does, it's what God does. Befriend all, help speak to everyone in an encouraging way, in an uplifting honest truthful way. That's expressive and detailed and understandable, for it all comes back down to, you really never know when the last time will be when you will speak to someone. So speak what your heart feels, what you know is in their best interest to hear, even if they may get upset, sometimes it is necessary, for everyone is so precious and dear, that they deserve to know the truth. If something is wrong, if they or you need help, just ask or simply do it. For life is too precious to be wasted foolishly. Is to precious to not accomplish something. To tell someone something. Do it now, not later, for later isn't

promised. Be right with yourself, others, and God, and know happiness will always be yours.
—*J. Michael Dekle*

Find God

The only way to find God is to search and try your hardest to find Him.
For then all of your heart will be searching;
So He will be able to connect to you easier,
For you're focused on Him,
Thus tuned in to His voice.
Once you begin to learn more of God and truly find Him,
You will begin to love Him and want to freely follow His commandments,
For they make sense to,
For they only make you a better you,
But also more kind,
True spirited, forgiving, relaxed, cheerful, outgoing, polite, honest, focus, sweet, loving, merciful, open, straight,
And an overall genuine person, that having God be apart of your life will totally transform you into the most beautiful person you truly can be,
For God knows you,
Loves you, and just wants to take those baby

steps with you, so you can truly know Him
too.
—*J. Michael Dekle*

Clear Vision

There comes a time—
A place—
A point in life where you reach where—
When you look out and onto something,
Your eyes see with powering vision what's
truly possible,
And the steps it takes to get there for within
those eyes,
Age, and experience lay.
Thus blueprints of unknown numbers do to
also.
—*J. Michael Dekle*

Going Through Changes

When going through changes,
Nothing's wrong with the new updated version
of you as long as you still recognize yourself
once the transformation is accomplished.
As long as you can justify the changes—
As long as morals and principles are a part of
it, the changes are worth it.
Whatever the changes may be then,
Will be a good change.
And if any around you dislikes it.
Pay them no attention.
For as long as what you stand for is good,
Is of love,
Of God.
They really shouldn't be hating,
But wondering how such a change even
happened?
—*J. Michael Dekle*

Past |Present | Future

The past,
Present and future all tie into the common
core of the present.
Leaving us to work around familiarity,
Which leaves most of us still stuck on
yesterday,
Leaving parts of today being sucked away by
the day before leaving progress slowly to
happen.
Making you wonder how can you make each
day a day of moving forward locking the past
days closed,
To reopen new door-days to file away
memories made,
Basing decisions off past choices—
Finding the only way to see things clearly is to
hold all three points of time together and look
through its filters to see what it truly is like
before saying anything.
Knowing it's not truly possible,
But the more I live,
The better I can predict,
For the more I understand,
The better I can connect.

Thus the better I can direct my life.
Leaving God as the campus and us the humble
followers.
—*J. Michael Dekle*

Different Shoes

I wouldn't ever want to be any differently,
really—
But some days I wish I could step into the
average person shoes.
For I feel like I may like it,
But then hate it,
For I would be so left out of reality.
For who I am now,
I sense reality better than most do,
At least I have to begin to think.
Realizing now it's just I have connected more
of it together then many.
If I step back into the past I lived and walked,
I step into the shoes of those who just haven't
travel on as far as I have.
Leaving, still I will never know some parts of
their reality fully, for I never lived in it,
But perhaps I at least touch enough of it to
say, I understand,
I feel you.

Me

For me,
It's beyond crazy to reflect on life.
To understand and see hands that touched me
That supported, helped, loved and shaped me
to be me now.
I thank my enemies.
I thank family, friends.
I thank God,
even the devil.
For it took everything and everyone to make
me simply me.
The being I am,
I can't say I understand fully now;
But one day I will more.
So for now,
I take one step at a time.
One day at a time.
Thank God ahead of time for giving me even
many more to come.
#LoveOn
—*J. Michael Dekle*

Windows of Actions

I look out my window of my mind all the time.
A lot moves me emotionally,
But so little does physically.
Leaving me asking,
Wondering why?
Is it,
I fought so hard for so long that now it takes
some real emotionally feelings to move me
onward,
To make me fight on through the struggles?
Have I become so heart filled with dreams that
it has turned me into a dreamer who only
dreams bigger and bigger and has forgotten to
walk on after—perhaps partly so.
Perhaps—
I walked so many miles alone,
That I refuse to move forward like this
anymore for I can't admire everything all by
myself all the time.
Maybe,
I have reach that bottom low,
And needed to,
So I'll know how it is again to feel rock bottom
feel again,
But at an older age,
So the feelings,

The company of such can impress me just
how important it is to stay moving forward,
And what happens when you pause and stay
there too long digging your own hole deeper.
Perhaps maybe it's a little of all that adding to
a soon huge enlightening moment,
And I needed to see just how precious and
important it all is.
Leaving me knowing each day:
It's my actions and decisions that will carry
onto the next,
Not the words said.
Leaving actions, the conclusion.
Your actions impact your future.
Your words are just inspiration.
Meaning they both go hand in hand,
Mixed in with faith and believe you can truly
do something great,
Just have to take step 1.
Then step 2, 3, 4, 5
Until whatever you seek is fulfilled.
Baby steps, daily ones.
—*J. Michael Dekle*

Student of Life

As I study others and myself more and more.
I can't help myself,
But to look deep into problems and even
sometimes relive them over and over until I
find just what went wrong and where it did
and from there how people reacted,
How my emotions rise higher, etc.
To answer why I do this: my curiosity drives
me, always wanting to know more and more,
plus it helps passes the time quicker.
From doing this:
This has only helped me grow into someone
more compassionate and understanding.
For the amount of harm my younger self has
done is beyond measure of words.
Meaning the sorrow I have when I replay
those invents in my head is a cup of grief,
Remorse,
A cup of reflection,
A cup of clarity.
Leaving me always wishing I could go back in
time to fix or say something just a little
differently.
For I know my words and actions have
crushed mountains or created them.
Leaving the amount of responsibility and

accountability that rest upon us all much
greater than we even can imagine,
For each word said,
Action done,
Is creating a larger bigger picture of reality in
both parties' eyes,
Rather they realize it or not.

Running as The Runner

Being me,
I can write anything.
I'm talking anything.
So I have studied and researched;
What do people actually want?
Believe it or not;
People like shockingly wildly crazy things.
Make believe, not practical things.
As in over the years the crazier, the better,
right?
The further made believed the better.
Recently studies have shown,
The educated thinkers, and actual seeking
people who want to learn,
Will rather listen to reason and logic,
Mainly because I believe so much make believe

has been made, that those who want to find actual life, love to study and know more about real world functionalities.
But there does come a drawing point;
They can only for a short time period—
Then they fall back to wanting to hear the crazy and senseless things.
Which is understandable,
It's a balancing point.
You can't always be critically thinking, your mind does need breaks to calm itself down, unroll and simply relax and take in some of that 'nonsense.'
Leaving me here saying it's such a simple reality to understand in the bigger picture of it all.
We have been taught not ever to be fully mature—
Maturity is a life long journey,
You never are stopping from maturing.
Like we have been taught to be free living robots.
How can you be a free robot?
Simply don't think,
Rather think what's already thought of.
Look how music has become stupid as can be,
Repetitive and shallow.
For people listen to music all the time,

So they don't really think anything on an
important level,
Just shallow more or less.
Movies have become so unreal that it leaves
you feeling emotionally empty in real reality.
News media has become so opinionated that
you truly have no right to wrong;
No guidelines of any form it would appear,
Just politically correct?
Who wrote such an instruction book then?
Mankind, but a selective few?
Forgetting the Ten Commandments that have
been ours for hundreds of years.
Gods since forever!
Leaving a society that has room for technical
anything to happen.
The people who question,
Those who still actually think for themselves
fully understand this.
And can do anything imaginable to folks who
simply are sheep and follow;
Saying whatever you will believe,
Just to stay hidden behind their lies.
Once you understand this fact;
You realize we live with children in control in a
lot of aspects.
Just monsters.
Leaving me to say,

Well, what should I do?
Be the adult?
Or be right smack in the middle so I can blend
in?
It's frustration as can be,
Period!
For to be an adult;
Leaves me way beyond my peers,
I'm talking leaving them decades away some
days—
We are talking my death bed ways away.
Perhaps not that far;
But some days I feel so.
Leaving me to be me,
Anyone I need to be.
Leaving me,
A transforming human being.
Always trying to be honest,
Straightforward,
But loving and kind.
Within so, speaking the truth, knowing some
times the words I express you do not want to
hear, I never want to belittle anyone, but raise
them up to a higher level of understanding—
Sometimes I come across as that, i'm just
trying to enlighten, I am sorry if I hurt
anyone by my words, I never mean to, but how
else can I state it?

Wouldn't you rather be told straight then beat
around the bush with it all?
Sometimes love is harsh.
But know all that is ever said is out of love.

Key-points:
Don't be afraid to question things.
Don't be afraid to think.
Don't limit yourself from learning.
I must say,
From this, all could be taken wrongly.
Have fun,
Do those simple things even.
But always try to maintain a higher level of
who you are today,
A version of you that isn't yet even developed,
So your always growing.
I still myself act like a kid sometimes,
But when it's okay and acceptable to.
I don't enact that across all levels of who I am,
If I would,
I would be a kid.
Balance my friends.
Balance.
—*J. Michael Dekle*

Freely Think

With an ever aging age of innovation and
interfacing technology,
We are only becoming more reliant on its
abilities to do things for us almost magically;
A selected few actually are geniuses,
Coding and producing such 'magic' while the
rest simply fade away to a fallen pinnacle of
life,
The pinnacle being the next big thing they wait
for,
Always wanting to be entertained,
But so lazy and stubborn to do it themselves,
That they are told what to look forward too,
Instead of going out to find it themselves.
That after awhile there's no such thing as a
pinnacle point,
A magical point,
It's just simply a changing point,
To the degree it's hard to value anything,
because things come in and go right back out,
To the point, it's easy to suggest almost
anything imaginable so naturally to people, that
it doesn't matter how bad or amazing it is,
It's just another thing,
Nothing less or nothing more,
So more or less you become more

desensitized.
What I'm getting at is:
Don't rely so much on technology for life,
Rather use your abilities to think to help guide
you in life,
So you still have an actual mind of your own
to think.
Thinking is freely.
It always has been.
Have you ever had a passionate conversation
with someone you respect and love?
The time flies, the conversations usually go a
little deeper too.
Do that with thoughts.
Switch between thoughts and add to them
slowly.
Pause the thoughts down to dig deeper into
them if need be.
But find something you're passionate about,
and brainstorm it for hours.
Heaven for me is always my fall back,
For no matter how often and much time I
spend thinking about God and heaven, I never
reach an end.
It just keeps going on and on.
#LoveOn
—*J. Michael Dekle*

Special Time

Spending time with my niece and nephew is a
cherish-able moment,
For it allows me to see a reflection of my once
younger self,
Plus just kids in general are always so
unpredictable.
They are so adorably cute,
With themselves growing and becoming more
into who they will be is such a special time to
witness.
Always put family first,
For in the end they are the only ones who
count.
For the love is unconditional.
—*J. Michael Dekle*

We Come

We come and breathe.
We see what we must believe underneath.
Then look at God, then speak.
See me and see an instrument inspired to
climb a tower higher than this world has even
to offer.
Me off though lower than the earths core,
Pour soul told heartfelt words to see who still
has such a touch to them.
Many fallen down low shallow to wallow in
some emotion when I'm here swallowing in all
emotions given.
Taking mastering, combining singing,
rewinding doing what only few can.

Which is to stand as a fallen human being,
But believing as long as I have another breath
that I'll thrust another launch towards
bettering—
Holding out gold in words.
Protected by the Almighty,
Standing behind me and in front of me,
Surrounded,
A beckon high-beam light leaving only those
seeking to hear and see the messages.
Leaving the rest to see this as nothing.

Leaving me seeing even deeper than ever that I
must stand and shout out lugs full of heartfelt
pain,
Heartfelt truth!

Same man as any —

But touched differently than many.
Leaving me seen as insane,
But the true and wise will see I'm holding all I
have been bestowed with,
With saner than sane hands.

For we live in an upside down world.
Leaving the visionaries to puzzle the pieces of
confusion together,
So once we try to better we must go from the
bottom up,
So we will even understand it ourselves.

As we interact and dwell in such a hell hole,
We will glide through sadden,
Madden, heartbroken.
For when we open our eyes,
We don't just see.
We see and see through it all to back to when it
once was the golden days.
Leaving us understanding fully just how far
fallen we have hit—
How the fallen days have been our walk and

talk now for a while.
Now no longer shall we hide it.
But walk it—

Proud, we know of it.
Rather than hiding behind it lost in its
confusion.
Now we fly as the healers and heroes leading
onward upward heavenward.
—J. Michael Dekle

Launch Pad

As you see yourself approaching a launching
pad.
It somewhat makes you sad,
But of course insanely glad.
For you know everything will change,
Change for the better.
But if you always versioned it a certain way,
And see it won't be that way,
That's when the sadness comes.
Life's full of surprises.
Life's an adventure.
I welcome it.
For I vision and see only blue prints.
Blue prints sometimes change,
But usually, they only do slightly.
If they do dramatically,
Usually that means some new epiphany or
something tragic takes place.
We don't know what tomorrow holds,
But we can have faith that whatever it is,
We will face it with smiles.
For we choose to stay positive.
For its good for our wellness,
Our happiness.

—J. Michael Dekle

Success

My dream one day is to be able to travel
anywhere anyway any day with my family.
The dream is so to possible.
It excites me beyond words.
Yet saddens me.
To not have a family as my own.
For what's life with being so blessed with
wisdom and knowledge that nothing really is
ever impossible,
If you can't share it with anyone in a personal
affectionate way?
Success equals sharing.
For sharing is caring.
Sharing is loving.
You can love yourself,
But after awhile,
Yourself just doesn't cut it.
For it's human nature to share.
Have you ever shared something?
And felt bad about it?
Probably not.
So what's success without sharing it with loved
ones?
Success equals love ones.
—J. Michael Dekle

Never Let Go of Life

Even if it hurts,
Sometimes you can't let go,
You just can't,
For life has so much to offer,
That if you are true to yourself,
You would never let go freely of such
possibilities,
For you know deep down you never would let
go of your dreams,
So how could you let go of something that
adds life to you even if in the moment it
doesn't, you don't,
For it will as time passes.
So stay grounded in life;
That's truly being genuine.
Simply by living life freely.
—J. Michael Dekle

Past Relived

They say the past relives itself;
The truth is it does.
It lives it through other people who are naive,
Through even yourself.
Anything bad of the past always reappears,
For the devil attacks the strongest most
brilliant;
Yet most emotionally wrecked and damaged
souls,
For he knows,
They are the leaders,
The people capable of changing,
But since they are wrecked they can be pushed
into a hell of their own making by simply a
few guided words of suggestion;
To the point they're destroyed mentally,
emotionally and spiritually—
Their lack of belief in a better day and a more
positive world disappears,
For they only see and feel is pain, and
heartache to the point they feel nothing,
So they do drugs just to move the day away,
while they slowly simply fade away until one
day they wake up to reality and hate themselves
so much that they became entrapped even
again, but further,

For they lack confidence in themselves to push
on out of the hell hole.
The end conclusion is:
Unless God is in your life to guide you,
Your life will always be a roller-coaster,
because you're using your own guidance,
Your own emotional feelings,
Leaving you blinded for you can't possibly
know five years from now,
But God does.
So trust Him,
And know life will always in the end be the
best it ever possible could have been,
For God was next to you guiding you onward
homeward to heaven by each step stepped.
So step,
Step,
Step I go on heavenward—
Gods guiding, He's by me, helping me,
Who's following God?
For God is by us all if we allow Him to be.
—*J. Michael Dekle*

Emotions Realities

Emotions can be anyone's downfall or rise up,
for they are so apart of human beings that if
emotions didn't exist the whole idea form of
creativity wouldn't exist for anybody,
And we wouldn't feel the need to change
anything about our reality.
We simply wouldn't feel anything.
So there would be no need for much.
We would become emotionless,
Which would mean—
Robotic machines.
Emotions allow us to live.
Allow us to feel life's precious moments.
Allow us to cherish moments with realness.
Balance your emotions,
Or your emotions will run you,
Rather help you enjoy life.
—*J. Michael Dekle*

The True Way

The way of the many usually isn't the way of
the strange,
Different,
Great and golden—
The way of the patient,
Loyal, Royal,
Honorable and heroically hidden—
Is the way of the bravest, truest,
The kindest,
And most forgiving, —
Giving them grace,
Mercy and love,
Thus giving a sense of peace once
encountered,
That trust and friendship forms almost
instantly;
Leaving if fully true as a genuine person—
Having humbleness to the core,
Being open to the Word,
Having fellowshipping with God,
It will tell you their soul—
For to fully enact such a precious person.
One must know God to do so.
Leaving, they walk the true way,
For love is their way.

Flooded Emotions

Once you let your emotions float to the point
life's a blur.
You're in a dangerous spot.
For you are letting yourself reach a point of
complete rock bottom emotionally.
Once you pull yourself together and adjust a
few things you'll see life clearly again.
Giving life a balancing point.
Let your emotions settle so you understand
why you feel what you feel.
It's okay to feel things, to let your emotions
express deeper meanings to your life.
Just watch you don't live in a negative emotion
for too long.
Life will throw you problems,
Your emotions help you understand what your
is heart feeling.
Life will through you positive emotions too,
don't be afraid of emotions.
Try to understand them, so you understand
yourself clearer, thus understand God better.
Your mind helps you conclude it all into a
logical sounded moment.
Balance it all,
So life isn't a roller coaster, rather an adventure
that you control how you react to.

Real Than Realer

The realer you are with yourself,
The clearer you see yourself,
For your gutting yourself out emptying its
purity,
Its garbage, Its potential,
Its surrounding walls,
Giving you a sound perspective that can talk
beyond mountains leaving you with a mirror
of your own painting in a marvelous
multilayered spotted crystal clear beauty of a
picture,
For it's all of you hiding nothing,
But opened shining your all.
Be realistic,
Be real with yourself before expecting others
to be real also.
Don't be afraid to listen to others opinions and
perspectives towards you.
For they see things you do not see.
Find those you can rely on and trust to give
such feedback, but reach out and ask for it.
We all learn in different ways,
Nothing is wrong with this.
Most learn the hard way, but sometimes we
don't have to if we will simply pause and listen.
Be the realer than real person.

Stay genuine always.
The truth sets you free,
Be willing to listen to someones truth towards
you, and hope in return they will listen to the
truth you see in them.
We can help shape each other into better
loving God fearing people if we will allow our
pride to drop and let our love grow and
become all of us in every way possible of the
word love.
—*J. Michael Dekle*

Talent

Everyone has talent.
Many just simply underestimate themselves.
Find your talent,
And only become better at it.
We all have hidden talents.
Take me as a writer—
I used to be horrible,
Now I can't say I'm perfect,
But I am surely better.
Practice makes perfection.
Practice, practice, practice till you are the
master of it.
—*J. Michael Dekle*

Champions

We are the champions,
For we never will give up until our last breaths.
Making us champions of life.
We never giving in to life, but fighting it!
No matter if bad weather or good comes.
We still will stay loving life, and God.
Living honorable.
Us champions are us who follow our passions.
We come in all different sizes and perspectives.
We all have our duties to fulfill.
Each day we want to give up,
But we don't, for our passion is that strong,
That failure isn't an option,
It isn't in our vocabulary.
Us champions are us who stay genuinely us.
May all become champions of their passions.
May all follow God, for God is the one who
gives us our passions.
May we all fulfill the shoes we have been
bestowed with.
#LoveOn.
—*J. Michael Dekle*

Age 20

Wake up February 12, 3:46 am, 2016.
Saying man,
I made it to age 20!
Whoa whoa!
Jonathan Michael Dekle made it.
How would you imagine I would make it to
that?
Age 13 to age 16 told myself life was
worthless.
Now seeing just how life is so precious.
Thanking God, He lead all the way,
Even in those dark times.
Feeling more alive than ever,
Feeling brighter,
More connected and closer to reality than ever.
Seen so many lessons happen in real life
already to say maybe I already lived twice.
Blessed beyond blessed.
Still exploring more and more trying to
connect the doorways.
Wondering yet how things work.
Not perfect in any way of the word.
Know the difference between the world,
And actual true life,
Heaven wise.
Look to the wise to help open my eyes.

Surprised always, but loving it.
Maintaining useful knowledge rather than
uselessly.
I should be used to this.
As in life:
I have learned life is all about learning and
gaining better understanding to why things are
the way they are, why connecting to those
around you is truly important to do.
Leaving a footprint in time that only has your
DNA tracks imprinted into it.
Finding a deeper sense of peace, by adding
God to my life.
Living motto wise:
Live Free or Die Hard Trying Giving Peace to
All.
Honestly can say I feel no older, and feel age
for the moment doesn't have any hold of me,
That I'm golden.
Prime age entry to eternally.
Still connecting the puzzle pieces.
Seeing the pieces will never end.
Wondering if within if I can ever connect
them….
Knowing my mind will forever spin.
Saying it has to be a curse but write another
verse and say maybe it's not.
Know if I put my mind to it I could be an

astronaut, a denies, or perhaps another genius,
but priding down and saying it's only because
of Jesus.
Humble opinion to my perspectives.
Only trying to protect what I perceive as Just,
As precious…
Walking the fine line,
Printing the lines even further.
Age 20….
But haven't yet even started to begin to live yet
really.
To the past, present & future me!
Happy Birthday Jonny
Haha :)
!

—J. Michael Dekle

Gods Hand

It's wild,
So wild.
I never knew just how much of a poet I was
until I sat down and started to read others
writings.
For years,
I'm talking years and years,
I wrote,
But never read—

Unless it was informative information via
newspaper or someway online.
I listened to mass amounts of music,
Surely helping on a poetic level,
No doubt,
But still—
Now as I read the content given to write,
I'm beyond measure blown away.
For to write so heartfelt words,
Only God could inspire such inspiration,
Leaving a whole other reality to appear.
God directly is behind every action;
Good or bad if we allow Him in to direct.
For He can take anything and turn it into gold.
—*J. Michael Dekle*

Pure Reality

It's hard to calculate true reality.
For everyone sees things differently,
But even though that may be the case,
There are rules and guidelines to help us
maintain a moral compass on an overall view
and understanding of what true reality is.
Reality has many factoring pieces that conduct
what true reality is,
Leaving many not waking up to reality,
Because the reality connecting them and actual

life,
Is too much for them to handle and bear.
Desire,
Destiny,
Passion,
Love,
God,
Emotions,
Actions,
Location,
And forward advancement ties into reality,
Plus, much more.
There's different levels of reality,
The past, present and future.
Which reality do you lean on the most on?
—J. *Michael Dekle*

Choose

I like to think in some since it those who's lives
are the messes and begin to see just how messy
it is,
Are the ones who then in return,
Turn their lives around into something
remarkable.
That's how God is too;
He sees you as you are,
And always sees the potential in you,
Meaning He always sees you as so incredibly

special that to Him you're always a treasure.
I see it this way.
We all are so young in reality,
That we haven't even begun to truly grow,
meaning if you have Jesus,
You have eternity,
Meaning we literary haven't even taken our
firsts breathes,
Our first steps,
Our first anything really,
For once we choose Jesus,
We truly have chosen a life filled with growth,
And unknown potential,
That we don't even know an atom of what
Jesus truly sees when He sees us.
For me,
That's powerful and makes me never
underestimating myself,
For the saying is so true.
If you have Jesus,
You can do anything!
—*J. Michael Dekle*

Questions

If your someone like me:
You literally have something to say about all
aspects of life,
Questioning all things,
Searching until conclusion are found,
That it makes you almost adaptable to all
outcomes,
So at the end of the day,
It leaves you just a little less clueless,
And empty and slowly more and more
experienced and filled with actual life.
Question life, so as you question you slowly
learn of life.
—*J. Michael Dekle*

Special

What makes something special is connecting
the moment into a deeper sense of it—
When your mind focuses on what's happening
and then reacts towards it connecting
emotional feelings,
It's helping to bring the moment alive,
Allowing you to admire and adore each
moment happening,
Seeing the small little details,
So viewing a picture being made by each action
and passion acted,
That once all is connect, it makes it special and
memorable, that it is truly mesmerizing.
For the gift of life by God in itself is
incredibly special,
If you think about it deeply,
Everything,
And everyone has something special to be
seen,
You just have to take a moment to notice it.
—*J. Michael Dekle*

The Giver

Being a creator is awesome!
Like,
Yes, you do have some limitations,
But the limitations usually are those that are
yet to be found,
Or by what you think people will think and
judge you for.
The second you say,
Well I'm just doing me,
And God is my judge,
All those feelings of what others will think,
Slowly fade, going away.
Each day remind yourself of this.
As you awake and are more alive than ever
before by this realization.
Your vision is clearer than ever!
For you understand you were created with
heavenly gifts,
And if you use them,
You can create even more gifts from the gifts
you have been given.
God's the Giver,
Meaning, if you follow Him,
He has so much to give,
That you will never be empty inside,
Rather more alive than ever!

Slow Motion

If you slow your life down for a moment and
just think about time;
It's a precious thought.
People rush life faster than it needs to be
rushed.
Always trying to reach for that next desire,
That they miss out on the beautiful ones right
in front of them.
Blinding them from the blessings they have
been bestowed upon them.
Blinding themselves from the rights and
freedoms that are always trying to be taken —
Forgetting of the bloodshed that was given
just so today you could go buy your family a
loaf of bread.
Time,
Yes time,
It's precious,
But do you see it as that,
Or do you hide behind your own desire that
you forget want matters?
The technicality of time we are presented with
living on earth is:
One day you loose it.
So how do you choose to use yours?
Self-desiring wants?

Helping others first—?
Holding on protecting moral God-given
commandments—?
Advancements to a better tomorrow—
Living a righteous life—?
A la la self pleasing pleasure land to float your
life away to a no tomorrow end?
The choices matter.
You matter.
Time matters.
How will you use yours?
The things that last,
You can never find in this world,
Only things you can are people and loved ones.
Telling, your focus should be on them a lot of
the time.
Other things matter, do not get me wrong,
But God, Family & Souls equal
True Life.
Love On.
—*J. Michael Dekle*

Examine

We look and think.
Asking why we do what we do?
Going beneath us to find all of us.
Seeing each detail in who we are.
Wondering why sometimes we fall apart?
Thinking hard,
Seeing only God can keep us alive going
moving forward.
Heading onward,
Always trying harder than ever before to enter
into another doorway,
Knowing God is the only doorway needed.
Seeing beauty within all Gods nature.
Figuring out what life is truly about.
Looking seeing only hope-fullness.
With love as the doorway,
Everyday, every time—
Examine each perspective carefully,
To uncover life's gold each turn at a time.
—*J. Michael Dekle*

More

Usually,
If you have a little of something amazing, you
want just a little bit more,
But the more you have,
The less amazing it becomes and the more
normal it turns until it's too normal that you
need something even more amazing.
Be content with what you have,
And grow in what you have,
As like family, passionate hobbies and God.
The more of that you have,
The more life will be fulfilling.
—*J. Michael Dekle*

Connection

People have become so computer together—
So connected;
Supposedly in-touched by smartphone
notifications— sending signals of informed
information;
Off an icon named 'someone' that the
someone you never see, becomes slowly dead.
Seeing no facial expressions—
But only talking MSMing in person,
Connecting less and less,
For we supposedly are connected.
Leaving us becoming less personally together.
And more shallowly together.
Connect mentally deep.
And watch growth happen across the board in
your relationships.
—*J. Michael Dekle*

Beautiful Life

Life's peaceful if you find a way to be content
in the present.
Life is what you make it be.
So why not make your life fulfilling and
purposeful, uplifting higher moral ideas, trying
to walk those daily streets, God being your
Leader, you being the follower.
Living life soaking in all there is to thats
constructively healthy.
Finding lessons in all things.
Always wondering what's next....
Showing love to all you can the best way you
know how to.
Leaving life simply, beautiful.
—*J. Michael Dekle*

Example

Sometimes leading as the example is harder to
do than falling back and not being one,
but continuing maintaining such standards,
Leaves you as the example.
One that leads to better things can never stop
doing what needs to be done, no matter how
hard the times may be, so those better things
can come out unto others.
Being the example always leaves you being
judged.
But remember, only God can judge you.
So be you, do you, and do so with love in
mind,
And never question what others think of you
in a negative way.
Care only to help express yourself better,
So as you example on, you do so with all
having clear understanding to it all.
Example On.
—*J. Michael Dekle*

Wonder

If you're like me,
You have thoughts always spinning in your
mind.
Sometimes they are mixing together,
Making life just a bla-ing moment.
I usually allow it to happen,
So self can settle and tell me where I'm truly at
mentally.
Though sometimes,
Selective thinking is needed,
So others around you won't see just how much
life is screwing with you.
Or in other words,
How much your emotions are really
controlling you.
Control your emotions, and you control your
whole entire life.
—*J. Michael Dekle*

Up

When one looks up,
And sees a cloud and God is the first thing
that comes to mind,
One then is starting to see the bigger picture
clearer.
When one puts us into true perspective,
We are transparent beings,
Shining off characteristics of who we are.
Beings made special and unique.
Given talents to use to uplift God,
As in using them to help others maintain a
better experience of morals and values while
providing our best of living.
For God knows best.
Always.
#LoveOn
—*J. Michael Dekle*

Poetry

Poetry is interpreting life in a dramatic,
Empowering out of the box way,
That brings in creativity,
Imaginary with imagination that brings deeper
light that leaves someone mesmerize for
allusions and metaphors tie into it,
Thus leaves a million words being said in such
a short frame of space.
Poetry is capturing life—
And painting it in a beautiful way in one's own
language that summarizes the whole picture,
Leaving your own mind to sometimes
interrupt it in a million different ways.
Some poets can capture the very life of it all,
That no other words or thoughts will ever be
able to paint such a beautiful picture, and I say,
We do that with what our actions and our
words we say each day.
We give others the ability to sponge off what
we say and create their own relative projective
projection of who we are,
For what we say helps push buttons within
each other that brings in new realization of life
and self that it empowers them to do more
things,
By using their own interruption of what they

see it as
For they can relate,
And thus the story and life of poets goes on.
Of us poets out there....
I hope that enlightens your view on poetry,
On us as poets expressing life in the best way
we know how to.
And that you see just how beautiful words can
truly be to your soul if you allow them to be.
How our actions can do even more than we
know if we use our actions meaningfully.
—*J. Michael Dekle*

Priceless

Someone asked me recently how much I was
worth.
I told them I'm priceless,
I'm worth trillions.
They laughed,
I said why do you laugh?
They said,
You're not even worth $10,000.
I laughed and said,
Then you must not understand wisdom,
Understand love.

It's far more precious than anything.
My riches only gain more and more day by day,
For my love grows.
Yes, I have not mastered love,
But what I have mastered is the highest levels
of love I believe.
I'm still growing into my own words said.
After I said what I said,
The person walked away not knowing what to
say,
For they knew I was onto something.
Wisdom only comes from God,
At least the good stuff.
If you have love, and truly enact it,
You're worth more than anyone on this planet,
For love sets us free.
It's crazy how something so free is worthy of
being called priceless.
—*J. Michael Dekle*

An Idea

Developing an idea into reality,
Sends us brainstorming ideas away,
But,
Once you start placing the connections
together sensibly,
The magic of the miracle snaps and happens.
Until that point—
You only have possible connections floating
around—
Awaiting to be figured out—
Sought out,
Appreciated and seen.
So to add to the next connector piece so to
enable and allow it to join into the connection.
Or in other words:
To reach some higher level of understanding
to anything you have to connect yourself to it,
Plus the creativity behind it,
To fully understand and appreciate it.
—J. Michael Dekle

Flexibility

I love having flexibility in my life.
I love thinking and working in an intellectual
way.
But also in a still thinking way,
But physical.
Today's construction.
Tomorrow's landscaping.
In between media outlets.
Basing, pushing out positive vibes.
Authorship is everyday occurring.
If you can't have such flexibilities work wise.
At least exercise twice a week.
If not more.
Every day get 15 minutes of fresh air and
sunlight.
Think of an engine,
If you don't run gas in it,
It won't run correctly.
If you don't run an engine long at all, it won't
last as long.
Same with you—
If you don't eat correctly,
and just stay active
If you don't run you,
Don't try to reach more—
How will you be able to run sufficiently high

on all you?
Apply yourself.
And always never stop learning.
Transformation shall be yours then for life!
—*J. Michael Dekle*

Business Goals

Set yourself free from daily struggles of
limited income.
Become a business owner!
Either be the boss of your life,
Or have bosses of bosses all your life.
You'll always have a higher boss in your life to
some degree,
But why not be in the counseling room of
your business directing it the way you see
reasonable and your fitting of style.
A successful business gives something
perceived as valuable and likable.
You have to give to receive.
Always treat people with love,
So love is a part of your atmosphere,
But also a part of you.
Add parts of your passion for life creatively
simply into a business structure.
Money runs the world sadly,
But so does passion.

Be the passion.
The difference,
So love can be seen.
—*J. Michael Dekle*

List some of your passions below, things you purely love doing. Not all will be profitable, not all will be even possible at first. But if like the idea of something, see your drawn into it, say playing an instrument, go after it! No matter how old you are, you still can do it! If they bring you a sense of joy, a sense of purpose, they are worth seeking after. Someone once said something like this: if you can have passions that make you money, passions that you simply enjoy, and in the mixture of life passions like exercising, kayaking, hiking, riding, outreaching etc. your life will be fulfilling, meaningful, and welled shaped.
Shape your life.

_____

_____

_____

_____

E.R

As I sat in the E.R today for a poison ivy
encounter.
I couldn't help but notice how drugged out the
majority was.
How real the struggle was for some of the
others.
Yes, I only needed some small amount of
medication for my problem.
But I felt this calling of need with their souls
on a higher level they needed.
I couldn't help but feel for them.
Knowing once upon a time they were smiling,
loving life, then something changed.
Wishing I could just reach out my hand and let
them know it would be alright.
As I left, I knew just how blessed I am.
Leaving in my heart this desire to try my
hardest to help those in need,
For all they really need is a hand of love.
Someone who would just care about them and
let them know just how precious they are.
That all they really need is Gods love.
For its power works in ways we just don't even
understand.
—J. Michael Dekle

A Stranger

I swear I have had some of the best
conversation with people I hardly ever knew,
Because we have had clean sheets,
There's no judgment going on,
Only real talk,
Plus the innocent of each other is fresh,
Leaving surprises to pop out all the time.
Those are the real moments in life.
For there always so unpredictable and always
leave an impression of some sort that nobody
else could leave but a passing by stranger.
—*J. Michael Dekle*

Same Page

It's been on my mind for some time,
Just I have put it to the furthest place
imaginable in my thoughts so I wouldn't react
and take actions.
You may feel like I have been descent,
Which I have,
But it's because I simply haven't thought about
you guys at all,
For every time I did,
I saw flashbacks,
Saw problems that weren't fixable.

I felt I said a lot in the past,
And was rejected down.
As though what I had to say didn't matter,
leaving me to question,
If I would take the time to write something
with such concernment, and feelings,
You should say something back,
But you didn't—
Leaving free windows for separation,
To make it justifiable,
So I did.
Let you win,
Let you have your time,
To see what progress would happen,

And I was content on knowing I tried my best
to express my feelings,
But heartbroken not even one word could be
told back.
Recently, someone else did the same to me,
Left—
And said nothing,
Leaving me to question everything.
Later down the road,
They told me,
By telling nothing,
Was telling something.
The something could be so much,
For my mind will wonder until it finds what it
may be,
But by doing so,
It opens doors that if not controlled correctly
could turn to something that isn't so fixable.

I saw the danger in the act,
And had to reflect that back upon to myself,
To wonder if I would of done the same.
Leaving me to think everything negative and
positive to come to little conclusion.
Only that they had nothing to say,
Didn't even care to try to fix it,
To express its reality to them.
The past is the past,

It really is.
Within knowing that,
Now there is nothing to say of it,
For by now,
Nothing you say could redirect the way I view
you it all now.
Just it's lessons learned,

Now we move on.
We all our children.
The actions of the past points to that so
clearly.
But once you accept its reality,
And fully take responsibility for the actions
done,
The adultness in us comes out.
The realness,
And our hearts start to speak.
If you're trying to one-up someone,
Or be on top,
To fight your case with someone;
Nothing will ever be solved.
If you plainly talk and express your opinions
and feelings,
Then conclusions can come about,
Understanding can be accounted for then.
Until then you both never will be on the same
page—

Meaning it's a foreign conversation happening,
For the space to let the other express how they
feel won't ever happen.
Because in each others mind,
You are distant and on some page ahead of
them or behind them.
It's why laying down the realness of the
present in a situation is so important,
So you can jump to the same level of
understanding,
Which is back to the same page.
Leaving in the moment feeling to come
around,
Which is a beautiful moment.
Knowing you all are on the same page.
Open communication has power.
Deep personal conversations are very valuable.
Mature people have these conversations.
They drop ego for they see ego for what it is,
a monster within that makes you weak,
Makes you immature and childish.
The mature drop pride and ego and let love be
their power, for loves power is beyond words
to express besides universal empowering!
God is love,
Love is the sound of the universes,
Telling love should be in all things.
—*J. Michael Dekle*

Thrown Problems

Though life may throw you problems,
One can handle and survive on with God.
If you believe in:
'Live Free or Die Hard Trying to Give Peace
to All',
You won't go down without at least trying
your hardest.
The further you journey on in life,
The more spiritually, mentally, and physically,
you will become.
The more emotionally and understandably you
will become to live also.
Leaving each problem as an equation,
And each action as an answer.
Adding upon who you truly are as a person,
and who you are leading your way to become.
When life throws you problems—
The way you handle those problems at that
present time will tell you who you truly are
deep down.
Leaving you to ask:
Are you who you want to be?
If not:
Change is always possible,
With the realization of the problematic state
of who you are emotional, spiritually and

physically now—
Ask yourself is it acceptable and likable to who
I want to be, and become?
If the picture and imagine you see in the
mirror of yourself isn't all the way in your
likings—
Pause, breathe, reflect and take some time to
think about why.
Get a pen and paper and write down these
concernments.
Slowly then try to enact these changes in a
reasonable way, taking baby steps to reach
these new goals.
If you feel like, you have tons of goals you
want to fulfill, then again pause, breathe,
reflect and make a list of just a few of them
you would like to start working on now.
Perhaps it's one or two, that's okay.
Don't make your life more stressful than it has
to be.
If you can check off just one per month, or
perhaps one per year depending on the goal
size etc.
You still are better than doing none of them at
all.
Balance is always key.
—*J. Michael Dekle*

Energy Exchanged

Some of us drain energy from others,
While some give energy to those who can't
find it within them to push on in life.
Those who have a more stable condition on a
more positive level and more opened sided
spirit will always be sharing their energetic
sides by expressions,
In emotional actions.
Those who drain energy are the less stable,
And less open,
And less confident in themselves,
And more or less,
The lost ones in who they themselves are,
So they float,
Plugging in here and there to this person and
that person to survive on,
Forgetting God is the central plug we need to
plug into to sustain life.
We all are created differently,
We all need to share life's load.
Creating friendships that fulfill who we are
deep down.
Having family for moral and emotional
support.
But we all deep down were made to shine,
And be up lifters to all we encounter.

As we grow in maturity,
In understanding life,
We will fall and have times of rock bottom
feelings.
This is okay,
These moments humble us,
Tell us exactly where we are at, and more likely
than not you always walk away stronger, and
more matured.
The sooner you make God the rock of your
life,
The sooner life itself will be more stable.
Built your foundation on God,
And have a happy life.
#LoveOn
—*J. Michael Dekle*

Silence

Having a chance to experience pure silence is a
rare thing;
But when you do,
You tend to find it peaceful.
If by yourself surrounded by nothing but
nature—
And you try to think about really anything,
You will find just how much clearer and better
understood your thinking is,
For your mind focuses even more on the
thought.
When learning of God,
Finding that pure silence area to reflect,
Think, study and talk, is so helpful—
You will learn that the most peaceful sound
sometimes,
Is no sound at all,
For your emotions are calmed and not up and
moved by other sounds.
Allowing God to tell you of His wonderful
works in your life even more easily,
For your focused and have an open connection
to heaven,
With no static (no distractions) only pure
openness, pure silence, and pure peace:)

Mom

Dear Mom.
Who could have someone like you as a Mom?
Only seven lucky kids.
Why we call you Mom is because you have
always been simply a Mom.
In every way possible.
Doing the impossible,
Having seven kids without looking as though
you had one.
Yes, you did it.
Raised seven children,
Taught us all love.
From tying a shoe to making a birdhouse.
To cleaning a house to making a meal.
Yes,
You did it all.
Taught us God,
By enacting God's love.
Showing kindness to obeying the law.
Ensuring we knew what real work was by
working crazy long hours.
To coming home still working like a boss,
Looking like a forever flower.
Coming across as an angel.
Taking everything to heart.
Being soft spoken,

Showing love.
Living love as your motto.
Jesus as your mentor.
Telling all you couldn't do it without the good
Lord.
Being the humbleness of us all.
Never thinking about yourself,
Always being the selfless soul.
The soldier hidden behind an angel.
The prayer warrior that nobody ever knew of
But you did it,
Because you live to love,
Live to serve.
Give your all so your children can have all the
chances possible to live.
Even if they haven't yet lived up to all they
know—
You have such faith that it's as though you talk
directly to God.
Already knowing they all will be saved,
For you taught them so well,
That the seeds will forever be planted in their
hearts and souls.
For you gave the most precious gift a mother
could give better than gold,
God's love.
Yes, you love only as a Mother can love.
Such a love that it will be forever remembered.

So yes you did it, Mom.
Been the Mom we all hold as the most
precious person we will ever know,
Our dearest Mother.
So Happy Mothers Day!
May your days forever be filled with everlasting
love from us all and above.
Love you,
—*J. Michael Dekle*

Truly Impacting
Steve Jobs' Last Words

"I reached the pinnacle of success in the
business world.

In others' eyes, my life is an epitome of
success.

However,

Aside from work,

I have little joy.

In the end,

Wealth is only a fact of life that I am
accustomed to.

At this moment,

Lying on the sick bed and recalling my whole
life,

I realize that all the recognition and wealth
that I took so much pride in,

Have paled and become meaningless in the
face of impending death.

In the darkness,

I look at the green lights from the life
supporting machines and hear the humming
mechanical sounds,

I can feel the breath of god of death drawing
closer…

Now I know,

When we have accumulated sufficient wealth

to last our lifetime,
We should pursue other matters that are
unrelated to wealth…

Should be something that is more important:
Perhaps relationships,
Perhaps art,
Perhaps a dream from younger days …
Non-stop pursuing of wealth will only turn a
person into a twisted being,
Just like me.

God gave us the senses to let us feel the love
in everyone's heart,
Not the illusions brought about by wealth.
The wealth I have won in my life I cannot
bring with me.
What I can bring is only the memories
precipitated by love.
That's the true riches which will follow you,
Accompany you,
Giving you strength and light to go on.
Love can travel a thousand miles.
Life has no limit.
Go where you want to go.
Reach the height you want to reach.
It is all in your heart and in your hands.

What is the most expensive bed in the world? -
"Sick bed" …
You can employ someone to drive the car for
you,
Make money for you but you cannot have
someone to bear the sickness for you.
Material things lost can be found.
But there is one thing that can never be found
when it is lost –
"Life".
When a person goes into the operating room,
he will realize that there is one book that he
has yet to finish reading –
"Book of Healthy Life".
Whichever stage in life we are at right now,
With time,
We will face the day when the curtain comes
down.
Treasure Love for your family,
Love for your spouse,
Love for your friends...
Treat yourself well.
Cherish others.
Material possessions can't be taken to your
death bed but memories will last forever in
your mind
Have a great week"
—*Steve Jobs*

Steven Paul
"Steve" Jobs
(February 24, 1955 – October 5, 2011)
(Died age 56)
Was an American information technology
entrepreneur and inventor.
He was the co-founder, chairman, and chief
executive officer (CEO) of Apple Inc.;
CEO and majority shareholder of Pixar
Animation Studios;
A member of The Walt Disney Company's
board of directors following its acquisition of
Pixar;
And founder, chairman, and CEO of NeXT
Inc.
Jobs is widely recognized as a pioneer of the
microcomputer revolution of the 1970s and
1980s, along with Apple co-founder Steve
Wozniak. Shortly after his death, Job's official
biographer, Walter Isaacson, described him as
a "creative entrepreneur whose passion for
perfection and ferocious drive revolutionized
six industries: personal computers, animated
movies, music, phones, tablet computing, and
digital publishing."

Quote from:
Steven Jobs

Information noted not my own.
From:
Date:
July, 15, 2016
https://en.wikipedia.org/wiki/Steve_Jobs

L ive On

O ne Love God

V alue Life

E veryday Counts

O ver power Negativity

N ever give up

#LoveOnForever

Thank you for choosing to read another book of mine. I hope and pray you will be blessed by the words. Life's an adventure and we are always growing and becoming someone better. We all have been and still go through life's struggles. It is nice to know we are not the only ones in which many of us face such troubles all the time. For more positive empowering words: Follow one of my blogs Via **Instagram —**
@jonnyslifeview

@sirnightwrites

@j.loveforeveru

@swiftnewsblog
&
@godscall1
Thank You
#PositiveVibes
#HeartVibes